But now, we said it

But who said it? The ultimate Real Housewives game book. Grab your friends, grab your wine and guess who said these 101 iconic quotes!

I have loved the housewives
for as long as I can remember.
Every franchise
Every season
any real fan will remember the
scene the title of this book came from.

There are hundreds more quotes out there
These are truly my favourites.

Wow Bethenny, wow.

"You're such a f---ing liar, Camille!"

    A. Kim Richards
    B. Kyle Richards
    C. Brandi Glanville
    D. Lisa Vanderpump

"Take a Xanax and calm down!"

A. Aviva Drescher
B. Ramona Singer
C. Heather Thompson
D. Sonja Morgan

"When do you send a little family van for 6 people?!"

    A. Vicki Gunvalson
    B. Heather Dubrow
    C. Shannon Beador
    D. Kelly Dodd

"Who gon' check me Boo?"

A. Nene Leakes
B. Sheree Whitfield
C. Phaedra Parks
D. Prosha Williams

"He's got a sense of humour which he will probably need when I take my clothes off"

A. Lisa Vanderpump
B. Kathy Hilton
C. Dorit Kemsley
D. Crystal Minkoff

"Were people doing Coke in your bathroom?"

A. Kim Richards
B. Lisa Rinna
C. Erika Girardi
D. Faye Resnik

"Physically you are a dream, mentally you are a mess!"

    A. Lisa Barlow
    B. Meredith Marks
    C. Heather Gay
    D. Jen Shah

"This isn't my plate you fucking bitch!"

    A. Kelly Dodd
    B. Shannon Beador
    C. Tamra Judge
    D. Gina Kirscheneiter

"You're an insignificant asshair!"

A. Gina Liano
B. Lydia Schiavello
C. Janet Roach
D. Jackie Gillies

"Bye, Ashy!"

A. Kenya Moore
B. Porsha Williams
C. Kim Zolciak
D. Nene Leakes

"I've been through ups and downs in life but I've never been poor. Poor is a state of mind and I am not about that life."

    A. Christall Kay
    B. Lejoy Mathatato
    C. Tarina Patel
    D. Brinnette Seopela

"You know what I've heard about you? Not a fucking thing!"

A. Gilda Kirkpatrick
B. Louise Wallace
C. Julia Sloane
D. Michelle Blanchard

"I'm not stupid. I have Sky News."

A. Dawn Ward
B. Nicole Sealey
C. Tanya Bardsley
D. Lauren Simon

"Your pussy's too dry to ride me this hard, Manuela."

    A. Gamble Wolfe

    B. Pettifleur Berenger

    C. Chyka Keebaugh

    D. Gina Liano

"You're a slut pig."

    A. Brandi Glanville

    B. Tamra Judge

    C. Kim Richards

    D. Nene Leakes

"Please don't let it be about Tom....." "It's about Tom."

A. Bethenny Frankel and Luann De Lesseps
B. Ramona Singer and Sonja Morgan
C. Kim Richards and Brandi Glanville
D. Stephanie Hollman and Brandi Redmond

"The only thing artificial or fake about me....is this!"
proceeds to throw fake leg across room

A. Kristin Taekman
B. Aviva Drescher
C. Tiffany Moon
D. D'Andra Simmons

"Her husband gets his dick sucked at The Round-Up. I know the boys who did it."

A. Brandi Glanville
B. Leenne Locken
C. Nene Leakes
D. Sheree Whitfield

"I make my own rules and one time I made dinner"

A. Vicki Gunvalson

B. Kelly Dodd

C. Heather Dubrow

D. Tiffany Moon

"CLIP!!"

A. Dorinda Medley
B. Heather Thomson
C. Sonja Morgan
D. Bethenny Frankel

"Thank you I am disengaging. I am not engaging."

A. Meredith Marks
B. Jen Shah
C. Heather Gay
D. Mary Cosby

"People come for me all the time, they just don't find me."

A. Karen Huger
B. Gizelle Bryant
C. Lisa Vanderpump
D. Ramona Singer

"You're gonna go with Mary, who fucked her Grandfather?!"

A. Jody Claman

B. Jen Shah

C. Joan Kelley Walker

D. Magaret Josephs

"I'll tell you how I'm doing, not well Bitch!"

A. Heather Gay
B. Melissa Gorga
C. Dorinda Medley
D. Mary Zilba

"She's a beauty queen on bath salts."

    A. Kenya Moore
    B. Phaedra Parks
    C. Marlo Hampton
    D. Nene Leakes

"Your husbands in the pool"

A. Danielle Staub
B. Margaret Josephs
C. Jackie Goldschneider
D. Teresa Guidice

"Honey, you are a slut from the 90's!"

A. Kim Zolciak

B. Drew Sidora

C. Porsha Williams

D. Kandi Burruss

"I don't throw wine glasses, I throw wine."

A. Brandi Glanville
B. Sonja Morgan
C. Christina Kiesel
D. Ronnie Negus

"I'm exhausted...my weave is exhausted...the panty liner on my underwear is exhausted."

    A. Dawn Ward
    B. LeeAnne Locken
    C. Kenya Moore
    D. Whitney Rose

"She will fart on command and I will dance in her fart!"

A. Eboni K. Williams
B. Kyle Richards
C. Stephanie Hollman
D. Kary Brittingham

"Whore! You were engaged 19 times, prositution whore!"

A. Teresa Guidice
B. Danielle Staub
C. Melissa Gorga
D. Margaret Josephs

"Want to know who your friends are? Get old and go broke."

A. Erika Girardi
B. Taylor Armstrong
C. Brandi Glanville
D. Teddi Mellencamp

"I will drag you, pregnant and all."

A. Monique Samuels
B. Candiace Dillard
C. Ashley Darby
D. Wendy Ofosu

"At least I don't do crystal meth in the bathroom all night, Bitch."

    A. Lisa Rinna
    B. Kim Richards
    C. Brandi Glanville
    D. Taylor Armstrong

"If you roll your mother fucking eyes over there one more time I will drown you bitch"

A. Jen Shah
B. Mary Cosby
C. Heather Gay
D. Brandi Glanville

"There is no comparison. Mine is a 3 wick candle, and hers is 1."

    A. Karen Huger
    B. Bethenny Frankel
    C. Sonja Morgan
    D. Dorinda Medley

"I had three weeks of diarrhea and vomiting because of you"

A. Teresa Guidice
B. Danielle Staub
C. Kim Richards
D. Lisa Vanderpump

"I hear the economy is crashing…so that's why I pay cash for everything"

A. Erika Girardi
B. Jen Shah
C. Teresa Guidice
D. Brandi Redmond

"There was the hair, I think it's extensions, and the blown up fake lips, but erm then I realised oh my god, that's who it is, it's Faye Resnick. The morally corrupt Faye Resnick."

    A. Dorit Kemsley
    B. Denise Richards
    C. Camille Grammer
    D. Lisa Rinna

"My mind goes automatically violent when it comes to convenience stores"

A. Mary Cosby
B. Yolanda Hadid
C. Adrienne Maloof
D. Whitney Rose

"Guess what bitch. I'm not threatening. I'm promising."

    A. Erika Girardi
    B. LeeAnne Locken
    C. Candiace Dillard
    D. Porsha Williams

"I've known Mia for 5 seconds honey, and I'm learning about her busted ass bean already."

A. Candiace Dillard
B. Gizelle Bryant
C. Karen Huger
D. Wendy Ofosu

"My labour is being induced because the baby is fully developed and he's ready to climb out of my vagina."

A. Phaedra Parks
B. Kim Zolciak
C. Monique Samuels
D. Kenya Moore

"Why don't you have a piece of bread and maybe you'll calm down."

A. Kyle Richards
B. Kim Richards
C. Eileen Davidson
D. Garcelle Beauvais

"Girl, them titties is aged hens. They social distancing. Bitch don't come for me."

    A. Porsha Williams
    B. Kenya Moore
    C. Eva Marcille
    D. Nene Leakes

"You are psychotic, Jesus Jugs!"

A. Tamra Judge
B. Gretchen Rossi
C. Kelly Dodd
D. Heather Dubrow

"Be cool, don't be all like, un-cool."

A. Kristin Taekman
B. Ramona Singer
C. Luann De Lesseps
D. Leah McSweeney

"I mean this is a crazy night, between the strippers and the grandpa fucking and the drinking, it's a good thing our mormon friends aren't here."

A. Heather Gay
B. Lisa Barlow
C. Meredith Marks
D. Whitney Rose

"You know what? You owe me a big fucking apology, and when you get on your knees and apologise to me is when I will accept you back as a friend"

A. Leeanne Locken
B. D'Andra Simmons
C. Brandi Redmond
D. Stephanie Hollman

"My hat is beautiful. It has green moss, little brown rabbit turds and a toilet seat, poop and a dog on it."

A. Brandi Redmond
B. Sonja Morgan
C. Marlo Hampton
D. Tanya Bardsley

"This is not glamping, this is full on camping. We have no ice, there's no counter space in the bathroom for your makeup and there's bugs everywhere."

A. Tamra Judge
B. Gretchen Rossi
C. Peggy Tanous
D. Alexis Bellino

"I married my first husband because he had a really nice ass and a great car"

    A. Tamra Judge
    B. Vicki Gunvalson
    C. Jeana Keough
    D. Kelly Dodd

"For some people, showing up at a bridal salon without a ring or a groom might appear bizarre and quite unusual -but for me, it's a regular Tuesday afternoon."

    A. Jules Wainstein
    B. Kelly Bensimon
    C. Tinsley Mortimer
    D. Leah McSweeney

"Where did you get this....? I'm asking you a question you dumb fat bitch."

A. Gamble Wolfe
B. Sally Bloomfield
C. Andrea Moss
D. Janet Roach

"My kids are dickheads. I hate my husband."

    A. Athena Levendi
    B. Lisa Oldfield
    C. Victoria Rees
    D. Krissy Marsh

"What are you offended about? That you were a fat little girl when you were little isn't that the reality?"

A. Krissy Marsh
B. Athena Levendi
C. Nicole O'Neill
D. Matty Samaei

"You're just an old woman who is pissed off and bitter"

A. Meghan King Edmonds
B. Alexis Bellino
C. Tamra Judge
D. Braunwyn Windham-Burke

"Is my vagina going to go back to my perfect little pistachio?"

A. Sonja Morgan
B. Kristin Taekman
C. Jules Wainstein
D. Bethenny Frankel

"If she thinks she is gonna be the star of my show, she is sadly mistaken"

   A. Bethenny Frankel
   B. Luann De Lesseps
   C. Ramona Singer
   D. Leah McSweeney

"You wanna be all this and all that and you shopping at Ikea and your shit ain't finished. Bitch get out of here"

A. Nene Leakes
B. Kenya Moore
C. Phaedra Parks
D. Sheree Whitfield

"Whoever says money can't buy happiness clearly doesn't have my credit limit."

A. Margaret Josephs
B. Jackie Goldschenider
C. Jennifer Aydin
D. Melissa Gorga

"It's not about me, it's about Kyle. Even though everything's about me, I'm trying to make this about Kyle."

A. Dorit Kemsley
B. Lisa Vanderpump
C. Crystal Minkoff
D. Lisa Rinna

"We were all so happy that day….it's….it's actually hard to even imagine how terrible things would soon become."

A. Kathy Hilton
B. Kyle Richards
C. Teddi Mellencamp
D. Lisa Rinna

"She asked me why are your arms so muscly? Because I back-comb my hair everyday!"

A. Janet Roach
B. Gina Liano
C. Andrea Moss
D. Sally Bloomfield

"There's a vibrator in the chicken!"

A. Leah McSweeney
B. Sonja Morgan
C. Luann De Lesseps
D. Ramona Singer

"I don't care if you're the biggest fucking heroin addict, prostitute on the street. I would never shame you. I would invite you to my house and say 'WTF is going on?'"

A. Dorinda Medley
B. Jill Zarin
C. Alex McCord
D. Aviva Drescher

"Who is Hunky Dory?'"

    A. Lisa Vanderpump
    B. Crystal Mikhoff
    C. Kathy Hilton
    D. Kim Richards

"Bitch, I elevate this shit.'"

A. Leah McSweeney
B. Aviva Drescher
C. Jules Wainstein
D. Heather Thomson

"You're going to see me. I look like a flapper with cankles.'"

A. Jen Shah
B. Whitney Rose
C. Mary Cosby
D. Heather Gay

"You are a mean girl and you are in high school, and while you're in high school, I am in Brooklyn."

A. Bethenny Frankel
B. Alex McCord
C. Kelly Bensimon
D. Sonja Morgan

"I'd blow Simon Van Kempen for a slurpee right now."

A. Ramona Singer
B. Eboni K. Williams
C. Bethenny Frankel
D. Dorina Medley

"Talk to my 6 carat diamond you bitch!"

A. Athena Levendi
B. Krissy Marsh
C. Victoria Rees
D. Lisa Oldfield

"Do you know what, I'm leaving because I'm not going to listen to this fucking bitch anymore, not one more word."

A. Victoria Rees
B. Lisa Oldfield
C. Matty Samaei
D. Nicole O'Neill

"I have a beautiful tan clitoris."

A. Ashley Darby

B. Gizelle Bryant

C. Wendy Ofeso

D. Karen Huger

"I was awoken in the middle of the night by two male voices....one was Luann's."

A. Carole Radziwell
B. Bethenny Frankel
C. Ramona Singer
D. Sonja Morgan

"You guys are drinking Dom Perignon 2003. In 2003 it was a heat-wave. Fifty-six hundred people died and it made for the best grapes of all time."

A. Heather Gay
B. Jennie Nguyen
C. Mary Cosby
D. Jen Shah

"I don't know what else you need to see, if you want to see Jesus Christ of Nazareth himself come down to tap you on your lace front. But I am telling you. She is not your friend"

A. Ashley Darby
B. Wendy Ofesu
C. Candiace Dillard
D. Robyn Dixon

"Are you fucking serious? I got stuck in a current and I nearly fucking drowned!"

A. Lisa Oldfield
B. Victoria Rees
C. Matty Samaei
D. Athena Levendi

"Gizelle is not a host. She is not a dresser, she's not too-good a wig wearer. I'm just saying."

A. Karen Huger
B. Ashley Darby
C. Robyn Dixon
D. Mia Thronton

"I don't know. She's an overweight middle aged woman. I don't think much about her. As soon as she figures out I not only stole her listing, but am going to steal her show, she's going to be pissed"

    A. Vicki Ginvalson
    B. Gretchen Rossi
    C. Tamra Judge
    D. Quinn Fry

"And while she's sitting around, running around talking about my husband and the father of my child, she spends her weekends paddling through sperm banks, looking through catalogues, trying to find a donor. Honey, you don't know if your baby daddy will be an axe murderer or a child molester, because what you will know is that he needed $10 to get him a medium sized pizza, so he ejaculated in a cup so you could have a kid. Now check that."

A. Phaedra Parks
B. Kenya Moore
C. Porsha Williams
D. Nene Leakes

"Ok, what you think is killing and what I think is killing are two different things."

A. LeeAnne Locken
B. Stephanie Hollman
C. Brandi Redmond
D. Kary Brittingham

"My primary source of income? My two divorces. I have worked very hard for every single penny I've earnt. I was married to two very irritating men, not for very long of course, but I definitely worked very hard for my money."

A. Jody Claman
B. Christina Kiesel
C. Ronnie Negus
D. Mary Zilba

"I am putting your ass on notice. Because what you are not going to do, let's be very clear, is you're not going to play with my husband's name."

A. Ashley Darby
B. Karen Huger
C. Robyn Dixon
D. Wendy Ofeso

"Seriously, you are a piece of shit Mary, you have fillers in your face and you look like a martian, YOU ARE A PIECE OF SHIT FILLER. You're a hooker, Mary you are a hooker!"

A. Ronnie Negus
B. Jody Claman
C. Reiko MacKenzie
D. Amanda Hansen

"Jackie you are all fart and no shit, I can tell you that much."

A. Lydia Schiavello

B. Andrea Moss

C. Pettifleur Berenger

D. Gina Liano

"I mean who is this woman? Coming at me with her pointy finger and her fucking camel teeth."

    A. Jackie Gillies
    B. Janet Roach
    C. Gina Liano
    D. Andrea Moss

"Paris Hilton taught me that. Just pretend you're talking on the phone, really pisses people off."

A. Danielle Staub
B. Teresa Guidice
C. Melissa Gorga
D. Jennifer Aydin

"You know what....no wonder why you cheated on your wife!"

A. Kelly Dodd
B. Shannon Beador
C. Emily Simpson
D. Vicki Gunvalson

"I am not going to hang out with Sally she can go fuck herself but I do feel sorry for her because I know she's grieving at the moment"

A. Janet Roach
B. Gina Liano
C. Jackie Gillies
D. Andrea Moss

"That glass of champagne just slipped right out of my hand ok, I didn't even know it was moving and it landed on her flippin wig. I don't like chaos, it makes me crazy."

A. Christall Kay
B. Naledi Willers
C. Mercy Mogase
D. Tarina Patel

"Wake up! You are a sloppy chihuahua! You're never clear you're wasted all the time so get over yourself!"

A. Kelly Dodd
B. Emily Simpson
C. Gina Kirschenheiter
D. Vicki Ginvalson

"You're over there looking like a white woman in drag, shut the hell up."

    A. Nene Leakes
    B. Cynthia Bailey
    C. Kenya Moore
    D. Drew Sidora

"Ooof, you are so angry."

A. Denise Richards
B. Lisa Vanderpump
C. Dorit Kemsley
D. Lisa Rinna

"I don't think she gets it"

"So you really think she is naive?"

"I think that she's stupid."

    A. Robyn Dixon and Katie Rost

    B. Katie Rost and Karen Huger

    C. Karen Huger and Ashley Darby

    D. Katie Rost and Gizelle Bryant

"Try me in a restaurant, don't try me in my house. I invited her into my home, I gave her a beverage."

A. Candiace Dillard
B. Ashley Darby
C. Wendy Ofeso
D. Robyn Dixon

"Yeh.....I'm drinking Luann!"

A. Ramona Singer

B. Tinsley Mortimer

C. Leah McSweeney

D. Sonja Morgan

"You are a fucking psycho you fucking pig bitch you liar fucking cunt!"

A. Emily Simpson
B. Heather Dubrow
C. Kelly Dodd
D. Tamra Judge

"I mean I'm sorry that I said you were dumb, maybe I meant you were stupid I don't know, I don't know."

    A. Monique Samuels
    B. Mia Thornton
    C. Katie Rost
    D. Ashley Darby

"Wait are you saying my husband is gay? Cause he licks my asshole. Have you ever had your asshole licked? It's actually very erotic. Maybe you should try it."

A. Brandi Redmond
B. Stephanie Hollman
C. Tiffany Moon
D. Kary Brittingham

"Waking up in the morning, thinking about so many things, I just wish things would get better."

    A. Gia Giudice
    B. Amelia Gray
    C. Portia Umanksy
    D. Avery Singer

THE ANSWERS

1. Kyle Richards, Beverly Hills (B)
2. Ramona Singer, New York City (B)
3. Vicki Gunvalson, Orange County (A)
4. Sheree Whitfield, Atlanta (B)
5. Lisa Vanderpump, Beverly Hills (A)
6. Lisa Rinna, Beverly Hills (B)
7. Heather Gay, Salt Lake City (C)
8. Shannon Beador, Orange County (B)
9. Gina Liano, Melbourne (A)
10. Porsha Williams, Atlanta (B)
11. Lejoy Mathatato, Johannesburg (B)
12. Gilda Kirkpatrick, Auckland (A)
13. Lauren Simon, Cheshire (D)
14. Gamble Wolfe, Melbourne (A)
15. Kim Richards, Beverly Hills (C)
16. Bethenny and Luann, New York City (A)
17. Aviva Drescher, New York City (B)
18. LeeAnne Locken, Dallas (B)
19. Vicki Gunvalson, Orange County (A)
20. Dorinda Medley, New York City (A)
21. Meredith Marks, Salt Lake City (A)
22. Karen Huger, Potomac (A)
23. Jen Shah, Salt Lake City (B)
24. Dorinda Medley, New York City (C)

25. Phaedra Parks, Atlanta (B)
26. Margaret Josephs, New Jersey (B)
27. Porsha Williams, Atlanta (C)
28. Brandi Glanville, Beverly Hills (A)
29. LeeAnne Locken, Dallas (B)
30. Stephanie Hollman, Dallas (C)
31. Teresa Giudice, New Jersey (A)
32. Erika Girardi, Beverly Hills (A)
33. Monique Samuels, Potomac (A)
34. Brandi Glanville, Beverly Hills (C)
35. Jen Shah, Salt Lake City (A)
36. Karen Huger, Potomac (A)
37. Danielle Staub, New Jersey (B)
38. Teresa Giudice, New Jersey (C)
39. Camille Grammer, Beverly Hills (C)
40. Mary Cosby, Salt Lake City (A)
41. Erika Girardi, Beverly Hills (A)
42. Candiace Dillard, Potomac (A)
43. Phaedra Parks, Atlanta (A)
44. Kim Richards, Beverly Hills (B)
45. Porsha Williams, Atlanta (A)
46. Tamra Judge, Orange County (A)
47. Luann de Lesseps, New York City (C)
48. Heather Gay, Salt Lake City (A)
49. LeeAnne Locken, Dallas (A)
50. Brandi Redmond, Dallas (A)
51. Alexis Bellino, Orange County (D)

52. Vicki Gunvalson, Orange County (B)
53. Tinsley Mortimer, New York City (C)
54. Janet Roach, Melbourne (D)
55. Lisa Oldfield, Sydney (B)
56. Athena Levendi, Sydney (B)
57. Meghan King Edmonds, Orange County (A)
58. Jules Weinstein, New York City (C)
59. Luann de Lesseps, New York City (B)
60. Phaedra Parks, Atlanta (C)
61. Jennifer Aydin, New Jersey (C)
62. Lisa Rinna, Beverly Hills (D)
63. Kyle Richards, Beverly Hills (B)
64. Gina Liano, Melbourne (B)
65. Leah McSweeney, New York City (A)
66. Dorinda Medley, New York City (A)
67. Kathy Hilton, Beverly Hills (C)
68. Leah McSweeney, New York City (A)
69. Heather Gay, Salt Lake City (D)
70. Alex McCord, New York City (B)
71. Bethenny Frankel, New York City (C)
72. Athena Levendi, Sydney (A)
73. Victoria Rees, Sydney (A)
74. Karen Huger, Potomac (D)
75. Bethenny Frankel, New York City (B)
76. Mary Cosby, Salt Lake City (C)
77. Wendy Ofeso, Potomac (B)

78. Lisa Oldfield, Sydney (A)
79. Karen Huger, Potomac (A)
80. Tamra Judge, Orange County (C)
81. Phaedra Parks, Atlanta (A)
82. LeeAnne Locken, Dallas (A)
83. Christina Kiesel, Vancouver (B)
84. Wendy Ofeso, Potomac (D)
85. Jody Claman, Vancouver (B)
86. Pettifleur Berrenger, Melbourne (C)
87. Gina Liano, Melbourne (C)
88. Danielle Staub, New Jersey (A)
89. Kelly Dodd, Orange County (A)
90. Gina Liano, Melbourne (B)
91. Christall Kay, Johannesburg (A)
92. Gina Kirschenheiter, Orange County (C)
93. Kenya Moore, Atlanta (C)
94. Lisa Rinna, Beverly Hills (D)
95. Robyn Dixon and Katie Rost, Potomac (A)
96. Candiace Dillard, Potomac (A)
97. Tinsley Mortimer, New York City (B)
98. Kelly Dodd, Orange County (C)
99. Katie Rost, Potomac (C)
100. Kary Brittingham, Dallas (D)
101. Gia Giudice, New Jersey daughter of Teresa (A)